T0196511

Expressions of Poetry!

"This is the love that we have for God and Poetry"

Roseline Dominique
and Jodes Elveus

iUniverse, Inc.
New York   Bloomington

Expressions of Poetry!

iUniverse books may be ordered through booksellers or by contacting:

iUniverse
1663 Liberty Drive
Bloomington, IN 47403
www.iuniverse.com
1-800-Authors (1-800-288-4677)

Because of the dynamic nature of the Internet, any Web addresses or links contained in this book may have changed since publication and may no longer be valid. The views expressed in this work are solely those of the author and do not necessarily reflect the views of the publisher, and the publisher hereby disclaims any responsibility for them.

ISBN: 978-1-4502-5195-2 (sc)
ISBN: 978-1-4502-5196-9 (ebook)

Printed in the United States of America

iUniverse rev. date: 09/15/2010

To the readers:

This book is originally written in English, but there's some of them, wrote in Cre-gilsh*, means Creole mix with English, and we have some other ones that wrote in four different Languages. We bet you will enjoy this book. This book wrote for adults only; due to profanities. We've been writing poetries for a very long time. That means we live for poetry. We'd published our first book in Creole, titled "Lespwa" in 2005, now we decide to come with our second book in English. "Expressions of poetry" fits in everyone needs: Spiritual, Pains, love, happiness, drama, etc. By reading this book, you would learn from it, because these messages are God inspirations. He Inspires every ones in different ways to summit his messages. Like in music's that you could feel the beats, and the lyrics; dances, you could feel the body language, movement; paints, you could feel the drawing, but in poetry, you could feel the vibe, the writing, etc.

Table of Contents

Dedications and thanks:

This book is dedicated to the Lord. We thank you God, for everything you have done for us. You give us life, protections, and strength to write poetry. We are so grateful by your grace. We woke up every morning to go to work and spent our free time writing this book. Also we thank our mothers who gave us educations, believe on us that one day we'll be ones of the best writers on Earth. Rosemena St-Victor, Telcide Senatus, St-Louis St-Victor, and Odes Elveus, we want to thank you for the suffering, and you're guys are not going to regret it. We also dedicate the book to our kids, Shiyetta, Samson, Melita, Telvin, Hansen, Dairren, and Hanley; Our brothers and sisters, who always support us. Lona, Celine, Stanley, Hugues, Dieunade, Odalby, Marie-Mika, Fedline, Carline, Sheena, Kevin, Ashley, Daniel, Delgado,

Why would we forget our best friends? Jean Nerva, Savain, Benius, Salusa, Rolkin, Marie-Flore, Edwige, Regina, Guerlande, Mildrede, Emmanuella, Mercia, James, Judes, Cathiana, Sandra, Claph, Michou, Romane, Lindsey, Carine, Gary, Johnny, and much respect for those that I don't say their names. Hopefully you guys enjoy this book.

Put that lady first!

If it wasn't for my beautiful life,
Why should I give her my heart?
I know, she can't be my wife
But, with her trust, I'll never get hurt.

I hope that she accepts my apology!
I know that I have done a lot to her.
She's the only one that knows me,
And makes me be the best one, ever!

I think that you just got here!
Let her tell you about me!
Excuse me, my dear...,
She's the best one for me!

She really cares for me
Every time I'm in trouble
I want to help that lady
Right before she'll go.

She's everything for me... my spirit, my soul,
And I wish that she could understand
Without her in my life, my body would be sold.
That's why my love would never end!

The first one who always in my brain
Because, she gives me nothing but affection!
I can tell you that I feel the pain
Whenever, I can't give her my attention.

No girls can replace that one!
Yeah, she made me who I am.
The only one out of the million,
She would never be the one to blame!

Fire

Every time I see you,
Pay attention to you,
Try to talk to you
To tell you that my love is true!
Your charm starts the fire!

By your side, calling you baby
Just like a happy pony
Till fighting for liberty!
My heart is on fire!

My heart is bleeding
When I see you're smiling!
I see myself swimming
Without learning!
I was just screaming;
Please stop the fire!

You came on my way,
And wanted to stay!
That sounded so funny,
But let take it slowly
Because, I'm still on fire!

Without you!

Without you, I'm not blind
But, I can barely see!
I can really walk
But, I have to use my cans!
Please, understand me!

Without you, I can breath,
But, you're my oxygen!
I could truly talk,
But, I'm speechless!
Where do you come from?

Without you, I have my appetite,
But, I cannot even eat!
I'm going to be skinnier,
If you don't want to be by my side!
Stop playing hard to get!

Without you, I have a lot of friends,
But, only when you transform!
I only dial your number
Every time I need to laugh!
Can you see how I feel?

Without you, I have the best job,
But, really painful!
Think about you day and night?
Now, I'm going crazy!
Only God knows everything!

Without you, I can live,
But, I'll be a dead man walking!
I play cool all the time,
Even my heart is hurting!
I want you to be with me!

Love

We eat, and drink every day
That we can survive, right!
How could you spend a day without love?
Let me tell you about it...
Love is patient, truth, strength,
Joy, peace, hope, support,
Respect, tolerance, obedience!
It's pure beautiful kind, positive,
Light, beside all these things
Love is truly life.
Next time you go on your knees
Tell God you love him
And tell your partners,
Friends and relatives
That you love them!
Finally, love has no explanation.
It's just love
So, why don't we love?

This is the love!

I try to be the daddy
That I've never had, really.
One that could show his feeling
And gives you everything
That you need to be a man tomorrow!

That's why I'm taking it slow.
I didn't want you to have a step dad,
But mommy changed her mind.
That's really sad.
Hopefully, you are fine!

Is he a good one to you?
Please tell me!
I'm here for you.
I know you'll be a man one day
To understand why I couldn't stay
To enjoy life with you, cutie!

But, you always in my mind,
And even make me cry.
You're the one, and my only one!
Who put the smile on my face...
Every time, we're on the phone
Changing idea and place!

I love you with all my heart!
That's why today I'm so hurt
When I see you apart!
Remember that you're my missing part!

By the sea!

I was sitting there alone,
Watching the birds flying away!
It was a beautiful day,
And the water was so nice.
I thought of making love in there!
But, I forgot that I was lonely,
Like an orphan.
By looking at the fishes...,
I saw you by the boats
Smile at me like an angel.
"Am I dreaming?" I said!
How come you're the first one,
Noticed me out there?
You took my hands, and kissed them.
I was so chock, and surprised.
That is a place of love!
I closed my eyes,
Just to feel it more
By the time, I opened them
He was gone, just like that.
Wow, that's what I said, wow!

A lady!

You always disrespect any women
Because you got played by a girl!
Stand here with your stupid slogan
Girls make you hate them like hell.

I want you to make the different
Between a girl and a woman!
A girl always here to play,
But a woman always finds a way to stay.

I want you to be a man
So you could understand a woman!
Don't you ever take advantage of them
If you don't want them to do the same!

Aren't you tired of choosing the beauty?
Why don't go for the quality?
Love is not a funny name,
So, stop using it to play game!

A girl takes your heart as a toy,
Play with it, break it with joy.
They don't care about your emotion
And for girls love is an old fashion!

Are you a real man?
Why treating a woman like a piece of nails?
I suggest you to stop messing with the girls,
Be a gentleman, start talking to a woman!

Will the real women, please stand up
To claim the right that you deserve!
Let the players know, you won't give up
Because you are the "Love reserve"

Temptation

So far away,
In my heart way
I see yon bèl jaden
Kote'm te ka benyen
Toutouni, m'ap penpennen!
Je commencais a prier
Oh mon Dieu!
Dis-moi que ce soir!
J'ai gagné l'élection
Sans aucun méprisation!
Por favor senor,
Te quiero que mi corason!
Let him be mine,
Necesito se amor!
Il est beau...
Li byen kanpe!
Fè'l vin pi pre'm bondye
Pou'l vin pale avè'm!
Male: bonjour, ma jolie!
Est-ce que ca va?
Female: You speak French?
Male: Oui, and English too!
Female: Sweet!
Male: May I ask you for a dance, please?
Female: Why not?
Male: me gustadia que fieras mi novia.
Female: Que te dice?
Male: hablas espaniol?
O dios mio!

Angel tears!

Every time, I start it,
I always see a drop.
I start it over
In a different paper!
A second one drop!
I get mad, and get up
To find out what's going on,
And it's not even raining!

I sit down again
So I could make my pen
Talks to the paper!
Then a third one drop!
Make it four, five,
Start harder, never stop.
Now, I have to check the roof
To see if there's a leak!
Everything is really fine.

I was only in the first line
When I give up, going get some sleep!
Damn... bed is wet.
Now, I get scare!
I get on my knees ask God
Then he tells me
"These are tears of an Angel!"

Yes, I run faster than my shadow
Just to be by the door.
That's when I see her standing there
Crying for the real love
That she's looking for!

Well, thanks God
for sending her at the right place!

I will enjoy her till my body gets sore;
From the door to my bathroom floor!
Where happiness will grow,
Love will be the real thing;
And I won't be scared to give her my ring!

Simple

I was walking alone
With God protection
When you came
To get my attention,
Till you questioned me,
If I love you!
I was shocked,
And started to laugh!
May be that was my chance
To do my secret dance
While I was enjoying life!
I sat with my emotion,
And used my passion!
My body started to get hot and cold,
Couldn't control my temperature,
Started to shake,
Because I thought I was dreaming.
My mouth was crying,
My eyes were shining
Like the sun started to rise.
That was unbelievable
Even incredible
To revive something so natural!
Oh my God..., it was so damn good.

Telvin

Tell me what I should do to
Even see my Son every day!
Let them talk, because I don't care what they say.
Voila, the love I have for you!
I'm your only Daddy,
Not the boy you always see with mommy.

Telcide

The lady who had courage to carry me!
Eliminate all her hates to support me.
Let me know how she suffered and she still
Care for me. I can't give her million.
I wish that I could show her how I feel;
Do everything for her, because she's the one.
Even thought she gives me hard time!

Only you!

Life couldn't be any different,
Not even in my dream.
I would take your hand
For any reason of life!
Right there, in that land,
I saw the end of my stupidity!
You were not the only male
And I wasn't the only female.
I got to know you better,
Then I secretly in love!
How could that possible?
Because I used to ignore you!
You had no place in my heart,
Now, I can't even sleep
Without dreaming about you!
You got all my attentions
And my hard feelings!
How would that happen?
Let me tell you that you win,
Even though, that's not a contest.
You understand, and love me,
Respect and care for me,
All these bring us closer and closer.
I see you as an Angel in my way
To guide me to my place
For a good eternity!
I don't need anyone else,
I just want to go with you alone!

My wish!

I wish my life was like a movie!
If I watch it again,
I will already know what's going to happen,
So, I wouldn't have to go crazy!

I wish that would be my movie!
I could play it, and stop it whenever,
While I'm playing it in media player!
That's how easy it would be!

I wish that I could know my destiny!
I wouldn't have to worry
With whom I'm going to make my family,
I would have time to set my mind free!

I wish that I could know what my son would be!
So, I could write, direct, edit my own movie.
Because I don't want him to be villain
Who doesn't have any plan!

I wish that everybody have a happy family.
Cheating and violence free!
Then the story line would change so quickly
And they would be no fake baby daddy!

I'm tired of wishing things that would never happen!
Like life is a movie... I meant movie;
Or put my Son and my mom's problem on me!
Because I really do feel my mother's pain!

I cried!

We started with love,
Having a great life!
We enjoy it together,
And that didn't go any further!
That made me cries!

You listened to your friends,
Treated me like an animal!
You acted as a fool,
Even forgot your idol.
That made me cries!

Your family said bad things
That gave me more strength.
There was no respect;
Like I was the next client!
That made me cries!

I tried really hard
To make you understand,
You pushed me away anyway
Like I was nothing for you!
That made me cries!

I even asked myself
If love had kill itself,
Because I need another chance
To make a good change
So I could stop crying!

My Queen

We don't share any tears,
And don't have any fears!
Smoothly, she talks in my ears,
And try to call me my dear!
That's what I call my Queen!

I could see how she feels,
I wish that I could make a deal!
With words, she could kill
The spirits that make me ill!
She's my beautiful Queen!

I really know that it's deep,
And, it's not a promise to keep!
For her, I could flip the script,
Even that I'm asleep!
Mad love for my Queen!

She always gets mad
Every time she sees me sad!
All the time, she keeps me glad
By treating me like her Dad.
Because she's my Queen!

If she has faith,
She'll be the first candidate
That I could take in the date,
Then make her be my soul mate!
My only one Queen!

She's going to give me a Prince,
You'll see only behind the fence!

Now, that really makes sense
To be with the Queen of the dance!
Thanks God for giving me this Queen!

Angel!

Walking in the forest
Where the birds take a rest!
I was all alone;
No telescope, no phone.
Then I heard a voice
That made my eyes moist.
When I got closer
You've already gone.
I ran all over, like a bear,
Hearing a shot gun,
I still cannot see you!
Then I went back to the street,
Started to ask if they heard you;
I could find no answer, till I quit!
Please tell me where to go
Because your voice drives me crazy!
Can you be visible?
So I could let you touch me!
Wow! I could feel your touch
By using your good hand!
I'll enjoy your kiss so much,
And our love making will never end.
There weren't any days, nights;
You control my spirit.
Let's doing it without a fight,
And I know we can do it
Because you're my Angel!

You're...!

The nose when I want to smell;
The eyes when I want to see.
Hands when I want to touch;
And, ears when I want to hear,
Because you're my pain reliever!

The heat when it gets cold;
The water when I take a shower;
Toothpaste that I use to brush,
And the cologne that I wear,
Because you're my lover!

The jokes when I want to laugh;
The movie that I watch,
Love songs that I listen,
And love poems that I always write,
Because you're my Super star!

The sadness when I'm happy;
The happiness when I'm sad.
Smile that is on my face,
And my oxygen when I can't breathe,
Because you're my missing part!

The dream when I'm asleep;
The joy that sets me free;
Beauty that pushes every men away,
And qualities that I look for,
Because you're the sweetest!

The lady that could be my wife;
The wife, I want to carry my next baby.

Life that I want to share;
And love that I need to split,
Because you're the girl I need!

Like you

When you have much to say,
You don't talk at all.
The day that I saw you
I thought you will never speak.
I wish to find a way
To avoid your look
That I admire so much.
You were so scared
You could even talk to me.
You sent your friend
To tell me how much you would want
To see me by your side!
Why couldn't you introduce yourself?
Don't be a chicken
That doesn't know its value!
To you, I am a little lake,
You don't need a boat to cross over!
I could you afraid of me?
The first thing you said:
Do you have any God-kids?
If so, can they be mine too?
That sounds crazy, and funny,
Then, I laugh.
I don't really blame you
Because that might be your best shot!
So, I'm not going to say anything,
Let me keep my mouth shut
Just like you!

Hear me!

You were born in the beautiful day,
Lived for twenty-nine years!
Now, you just go away,
And left me with some tears;
Without saying good bye!

I didn't even know you for that long,
But I still feel the pain.
In the corner, listen to your song
That could drive me insane
For some months, or years!

It's too early for me to go to Church,
Just to see you lay in the coffin.
Why, why, you had to be in the rush?
I'm still here, I'm listening,
And I won't go anywhere till you tell me!

I don't know why I should cry,
If I know there should be an end?
Let your body, and soul shy
Under this beautiful land
Where the Sun shines!

This is not how we plan it!
Now you've gone, I have to admit,
How would we be there for each other?
Now, you left me alone, forever!
I swear that you could hear me!

I think, it's not too late to write you this poem.
But, I just want to show you that I miss you,
By being there for your family's problem
Because our friendship was true!

?

You are a very nice person
Who fight for attention.
Don't you know life is precious?
Now, the nature becomes dangerous!
I know more than you think,
Let's go ahead, and talk!
It might be personal,
But, it's not the royalty.
I tried to understand
Where you stand;
Still, something missing!
Let me just ask,
Why this stupid game?
Gosh! It is terrible.
Too bad, I can't change it,
Even do anything about it.
Truly, I cried inside,
So, I could fake it outside.
I wish that I had the power
To make you be better.
Maybe if I was stronger,
I think I would stay closer
To save you in trouble!
Now, it seems impossible.
But, there's still a chance
To have a good time!
Just think about it!

Consequences

I feel the pain inside me
When I have to come to the Hospital
To visit your little baby,
She's the innocent one in the middle.

I know she didn't do anything wrong
For her to be in that situation!
But daddy thought was so strong.
Now she has to pay for his action.

Where's the love we're looking for?
Why do babies have to suffer?
From diseases and bodies sore
Cause of their fathers or mothers?

I know that I'm not the only one feeling it.
Other friends and families cannot deal with it.
Because it's hard to get over it
And seeing little "G" got sick with it.

The mother loves you too much, she decides to stay,
So do you care enough to stop the game you play?
I swear that I had shared the same tears!
That's why I'm showing my fears.

I felt good when doctor said she could leave
To go home where she belongs!
The only thing I could believe
Whatever you've done to her is wrong!

Feel it

With our hands,
Let us pray!
With our lips,
Let us sing!
In our heart,
Hold one truth alone!
Fresh water,
Fire everywhere...
Then, you would see God angels,
Move around us,
Worship with us.
Don't be surprised!
Just trust him!
He's the same Lord,
He doesn't change.
There shall be shower of blessing,
And it is a promise of love.
There shall be a season of refreshing
Send from the savior above.
Holly spirit,
You're welcome in this place.
Now, we could shout glory
Because I can feel it!

American Queen!

Pretty face, nice smile,
Sweet voice as a candy bar
Make me travel for couple miles
Not too close, neither too far.
That's an American Queen!

She walks as a model;
And I follow her like her shadow!
Short, big and so sexy.
Wow, she drives me crazy.
For me, she's an American Queen!

Her soft hands are fantastic,
Tongue ring is a fucking magic.
I don't know how she got me excited!
Because light skin girl never got me tempted!
Yes, she's an American Queen!

One day, I asked for her name.
She told me Andrea. Ain't that a shame?
I thought she was Spanish in that moment,
And find out she doesn't even have the accent.
Guest what? She's an American Queen!

I hope she doesn't have a boyfriend!
Yes, I'd like her to be "just the friend"
So we could have fun anywhere,
Especially in the back of her Pathfinder!
Then, she would be my American Queen!

Don't know

Thinking of being stronger
Run away from your lover.
You got me closer and closer,
And my heart made be a believer;
Need to say a good prayer,
Just to stay in your arm forever!

There was the word "never"
That controlled my temper
For me not to be suffer
For any stranger!
Something must come later
That's going to make me happier!

I had a reporter
To make the story shorter!
We are together
Trying for better
Like a secret banner
That has no after!

May be there is a danger
Warning in your behavior,
Like a virus in a modern scanner
That slows us down forever!
I want you to be my reminder,
Because I'm scared of a player!
So please, be a good driver!

I'm still by your side!

Anytime in your life,
You want someone to explain.
Don't forget if I'm here!
I'll be listening.

In the bad time,
If you need a hand!
Don't be scared to ask!
I'll lend you mine!

When you can't smile,
Always try to remember
That you have a friend
That can make you laugh.

When you're not strong,
Lean on me, I'll carry you on.
Because, you're my best friend
Till the end of my life!

Do you want a friend to trust?
Look behind you, I stand there
To push you when you stop
In the middle of your long way!

Those, I dedicate to you!
My poems and my soul!
Don't just read them, understand them!
Then tell me how you feel!

Strange

Maybe it's natural
Just like a little canal,
Trying to stay normal,
Not to make a big total!

The first time was something,
The second made a thing.
I felt like running,
But, my heart was saying...

... Something totally different,
Asked for some patients!
That was very difficult

Your body transfers electricity
In my blood with a possibility,
That is generally
Look so lovely!

My heart is on fire
With your desire!
I can just be me,
If I'm totally free!

I'm so broke!

I'm so broke
When I can't afford
To buy anything for my Son
Or help my mom, Telcide!

I'm so broke,
When I can't say
Hello to the society
Without someone
Hides for me,
And looks at me
As a junky!

I'm so broke,
When I can't celebrate
Happiness in mother's day
With my mother,
And the mother of my child!

I'm so broke,
When to tell the bill collectors
Who you want to talk too
While they're asking for me,
Or tell my landlord I'll give half,
And I'll give you the rest
In my next paycheck!

But when I realize
That I'm so broke?
Is when I'm looking for
My friends, I can't see them!

Remember!

Years ago, I doubt your love
It stays like that for a long time!
But, always get your attention,
Comprehension and respect!
I was your princess, your lady,
Your baby, even your sister!
You talked about me a lot,
And to me all the time!
I can tell you anything,
You always understand!
Now, things change,
In my critical situation;
Where I need you the most!
I counted on your support
That's now I can't find!
I sang, just trying to be happy,
I read, because I want to be stress free,
And I cried, so I could release my pain.
I wish that never happen,
Because I came to a door
Where I cannot exit,
And don't want to exist.
You couldn't prove what you said,
And I know it was too good to be true.
I can't judge or accuse you,
I'm still going to be there for you...
Just remember that I love you
No matter what!

Je suis Un Negre!

I'm so black
You can't even see me in the dark.
Un negre marron
Ki gen koulè chabon
Who fought for his Country
Qu'on appellait la perle des Antilles!
Now, where's the hope of my Flag?
The dignity of my blag?
Et même la puissance de ma couleur?
But, all I know...!
I'm a nigga who never give up.
Pour le Pays, mourrit est beau,
I will always keep it up!

N'ap di annavan, annavan...
Sa a se yon refren mwen tande tout tan.
Pourtant, on est toujours absent
Dans la ceremonie de notr'Ochan!

Porque tu no me quierres?
Porque yo no puedo habblar mi langua?
I could be so careless,
Men fòm goumen pou lang mwen sa!
Je suis un negre! Oui, I'm a nigga!

Let it be!

You tried to talk to me
To make me be your girl!
But, what makes it different,
We became something better.

You always remind me,
How you used to say how crazy
You would like to have me
Just to spend some good time.
The plan changed to friendship
Which never stop.
Don't force it!
Just let it be!

Things happen for a reason.
Trust me, you are the best one!
You show me sadness,
And treat me like a princess;
... Even take me out of stress.
I want to see your life
Full of happiness!
See! It is love... let it be!

I do understand your dream;
And we make a good team.
Don't you just stand!
Please, lend me your hand.
Com'on! We have a lot to do
That others don't want to

Because they don't believe
In opposite sex's friendship!
But, don't be foolish!
Let it be!

I cried so hard!

I cried so hard for the way my Country is;
While we're in the American's continent!
I continued to cry, after my visit in Ethiopia.
That is a part of our mama Africa!
I cried so hard when I take a look in the Ghetto
Where most of us live in the poverty!
I cried so hard when I see we cannot live in peace.
Even, cried harder when I see black on black
discrimination!

I cried so hard when I see kids in the misery,
Then, they're spending millions in throwing party.
I cried so hard when he has to do time
Because of dogs fight and they never do time
When they make people fight.
Are animals more important than us?

I cried so hard when I see any black's crime...
Is always a gang related!
I cried so hard when I see their crime...
Is normally a self-defense,
So they could release in the same day.

I cried so hard when the police got shot,
And they're here to serve us.
I cried so hard when the teacher
Had sex with his two females students
And never brought to trial!

I cried so hard when I cannot breath,
And don't have the right to live.
I cried so hard when we became so soft!
What makes it worse? I never cried that hard
Till Akon came out with the song!

No time!

We struggle every day with things,
And we can't even do anything.
We denied things we did,
Still continue on doing!
Questioned God...
"Why is me?
Why is now?"
Sometimes we need to back off,
Let him do his job!
Just talk, and sing to him
"I must tell Jesus,
I cannot bear
My burdens alone!
I must tell Jesus
To come help me,
And him alone"
While you have a chance
To see, listen, talk, think,
And make the right decision today.
Because there's no more time,
And this moment is yours!
I would like you to act now!

I'm a murderer!

That girl came up to me,
and ask me to be my girl!
I said yes baby,
Come to me, you won't be in hell!
I make her feel, she finds the man
That she was looking for.
But she never knows that a murderer!

I just wanted to get some that night.
Then she started to fight.
She thought I would make her dream come true
By being her hero. But she had no clue
That I'm a man, just like the other ones
Who treat females as the pocket of change.
Because I'm a murderer!

Girl, I wasn't here to have a relationship!
A brother like me is hard to trust you.
And I don't give a damn, if you think I'm cheap!
Because give you my heart could make me catch a
flu.
I know you had trusted me
But, I don't know why, if have no money.
I'm not even a good man, but a murderer!

We could always be best friends;
If you believe love made for us!
I know your feelings start, and never end
That why you're acting like you're overdosed!
Baby girl, why don't you stop crying over me?
Because it really drives me crazy!
Let me tell you that I'm a murderer!

Sorry for playing with your emotion!
I didn't want to be such a criminal.
When I got here, I thought I was in an auction
Where I have to bit till the big price blow!
You're the sweetest girl ever...
But, that's so sad that I'm not a lover!
I'm straight up a murderer!

Just me!

I could try o be normal
Look happy, and nice!
But hiding my feeling is enough.
All questions that I had
There were no answers,
Not just a single one.
I went crazy in my mind
Searching for anything
That could set me free.
Right there in my face,
They were flying away!
No one was there to help
Time after time, day by day,
I'm losing my confidence.
Do I deserve that or not?
May be it's a dot
To get to my attention!!
Who knows what is it?
Secretly in my heart
I'm praying to see you're there
To find out who am I.
I wish for better,
But I just want to be me.

Brain of a prisoner!

I started my day with a smile in my face,
And finished it with tears in my eyes
Because my relationship puts me in the bad place,
But thinking that I tell nothing, but lies!

Oh my God, talks to her so she can understand
That my heart can't take it anymore!
And give me strength to help her stand
When she's getting tired of my metaphors!

I hurt when I see myself took that decision
To be with a girl who doesn't care for me!
I love her, and want to take some actions
But I don't think she wants to be with me.

I would like to settle down with her,
Make her be the friend that I could talk...,
The only lover that I could take a walk
So, I could show her how much I care!

I'm willing to remain silent
Because, I was under warrant!
Now, my brain is behind bar, serving times
For all the time it was committing the crimes.

Please make her be the girl of my dream;
The only one who can make me screams!
The day she change her way of acting toward me,
That will be the day we will grow the big family!

For love or hate!

You could do anything,
Good or bad!
I get nothing from you,
Love or respect!
You treat me like an animal,
No life by your side!
You even tried to kill me
In front of the kids
Because nothing is matter to you!
I don't know what I feel.
There's no more feeling.
Is it love or hate?

Tried to divorce you,
Made me loves you more,
And went back to you!
It's really hard to choose
Living my life without you
Because of them kids lives
Without a daddy around!
Now, I hate you the most!

I don't know what to do,
But get on my knees, and pray
God to bless our soul,
And take control of the situation
For me! That's the only hope!

One night stand!

I'm in love with myself
More then I'm in love with you!
In the club, I was standing on your left
When your body gave me the clue!

Nice dress, just to impress
A gentleman like me!
You drink more, I drink less
That doesn't really matter to me.

I took you home to make my wish,
Or to find out if you're ticklish!
Body language in my king size bed...
Made me thought that you were mad!

You said no, but you needed it
Go ahead, and enjoy.
It's been six years, I haven't get it
So, take it slow, with joy!

You get me hungry, can I eat?
I will start from the feet
Just to make you Trimble,
Like you're in big trouble!

Open up, let me get in between!
Please do it like you turn nineteen.
We could also do it in the rain
If you don't want to feel the pain!

You left your taste in my lips
Just for me to ask you for more.
And you even left me some tips
Because I opened your door!

Thank you for being the lady of the night!
After all that, you told me you're all right.
Now, I would like to ask for your name,
And I hope you don't think it's ashamed!

Can't forget!

It was very simple,
Then you made terrible.
Accused me of your sickness,
That brought you more stress!
There was no reason
To treat me like this!
I didn't have to blame you,
Because it was my stupidity,
Made me say yes to your ugly!
I tried hard, and harder,
Even get on my knees to pray
Just to see if I could stand,
And move forward;
But I didn't have the courage!
When I called, you hang up,
Even ignored my texts
To make me feel dumb!
When I tried to face you
With your stupid lies;
You never gave me a chance!
I thought that you loved me?
Tell me what happened!
Never mind!
I know the Lord will show me the way,
And teach me how to forgive you.
And I know, I will get rid of you,
But, I just can't forget!

Psycho!

I don't want to convince you,
Make you think, I'm the best man!
I'm here to tell you that my feeling is true,
But, too bad we can only be friends!

I know that we're both singles
So, why can't we be together?
Is it because we don't like each other?
Nah, but we have dreams to follow.

But, I don't think that's a crime
If I call you mommy,
Or write you a poem with rhythm
While you lean on me, and call me daddy!

Truly! You're type that I'm looking for!
Because you have your head on your shoulder!
Baby girl, I know that for sure...,
I'm a player; I can't be your lover!

Yes, you make me say a lot of crazy things
Even I'm not there around you.
You're the sweetest girl who makes me dreaming
And even express my feeling to my all crew!

I wish you'd find you a good man, not a boy
Who will play with your emotion!
A man who will bring you a lot of joy,
Reimburse you up with his attention!

No more fear!

Satan attacks everywhere,
He brings all negatives
Things to our lives,
Try his best to keep us down.
But, when we call
The name of Jesus-Christ,
We change, bless, save, and protect.
He gave us victory by his death.
Demons in hell can't denied
When he says yes, nobody can say no!
So, stand walk dance, jump,
Swim, eat, laugh, and rejoice in his blood,
Because it reaches to the highest mountain,
Flows to the lowest valley!
The blood that gives us strength
Day after day
Would never lose its power!
It calms our fears,
Dries all our tears!
Things you are afraid of,
Are also scared of you!
It gives us power over enemies,
Sickness and all evils!
Now, with the confident we have
In Jesus, son of God!
... Let shout his name with me,
With no more fears!

The real me!

I used to hate the fact
That it was a part of me.
And everywhere, I used to go
It would follow me.

It tormented me for years,
Even killed my self-esteem
Of being dark-skin,
Wasn't so beautiful for me!

I used to fit in
By using fade creams,
Even bleaching my skin
To erase the real me!

African booty scratcher,
Tar baby and spook!
Blacky, stupid Haitian,
Just some few names,
Make me feel un-pretty.

And if I can't love myself
Who else who's going to love me?
And if beauty is skin deep;
Then my color is me!

Now I can see that my color
Doesn't have anything to do
With anybody, except me!
Oh my God, I'm proud to be me!

Mad

How could you do this?
I wasn't expected no careless
To drive me hopeless
Or make a big mess!

You said it to every body
That was so lovely.
Am I a no body?
Because that was funny
To see me playing shy!
Now that makes me cry!

You might understand it now,
And talk like wow.
Like there was no tomorrow.
I saw my own shadow
Under my beautiful pillow
Sleeping like a cow!

So, don't you ever tell me to be glad!
Because you are bad,
That made me sad.
Off course, I have to be mad!

Psycho 2!
(Female version)

I know we cannot be together,
But I don't need anyone else!
I feel as your sweet lover,
For me, you are the best!

In my dream, I always see you
Next to me and my dream never fail.
I don't think you have any clue
How you make feel like a woman, not a girl!

You're the man who fulfill my life,
And reimburse me with your attention.
I know you can't make me be your girl, neither your wife,
But all I really need is your affection!

We kiss, I suck, why would I hide my feeling?
If I could let you put it down my throw,
I don't really call that chilling.
I know a man always take things slow!

You think you're the only one who write poetry!
No, because I started it since I was a girly.
I also express my feeling to my crew too.
But they're always telling me to leave you.

They just don't know how I feel about you.
I want to be your best friend for ever,
Even that I know we're not going any further.
I love to be around you too!

I know that you said that we like each other!
In my side, I know that that we love each other.
You just not ready for commitment.
Good luck! Enjoy your moment!

Who cares?

The World these days
Has no word for kids anymore.
They say what so ever
What kind of influence?
Evenly their lives are danger
Then sentence will be...
Who cares?

They never understand
Why we try to protect them,
Want to push tem forward
With their education!
Well, who cares?

We don't have any choice
But pushing them hard!
That's the only way,
We can save them from trouble.
Pay attention to what they say.
Now people care.

We know it's not easy.
Still, don't be lazy!
Stay focus, and do it,
And do it with your spirit,
You'll se the different.
That one day, they'll care!

Black as I am!

Why they're all my upon my face,
Like my brand new sun glasses?
Make me feel like a stupid star,
Follow me with police radar!

Why am I always in the run,
Every time I hear a shot gun?
Don't you think I want to have fun?
And play in the beautiful sun.

Why do I have to use fade cream,
If I know black is my skin color?
I'm strong, and I only scream
Till the bullets drop me on the floor!

Why do you want me to change?
If I grew up with the slave mentality!
I'm not here for revenge.
But, stop making me feel as a "Slave to be".

Why tazer gun has invent for me,
While I'm not the most criminal!
And I know that I'm crazy...
So why would I be a denial?

Why the laws have to be harder
Every time I try to break it?
And their tears get dried faster,
Because they always get away with it!

Why they have to use the stairs formula?
Whites, Hispanics, and then me!
I know that I'm a nigga
And I'm really proud to be!

Scary!

We don't know what to think,
Even who to talk!
All I say... only God knows.
Come to Church, no one to look up too!
Hey, how could that be possible?
Too much is going on these days.
It's like we are invisible,
There's no one to give us any attention!
Things that used to be in television,
Became real action in life!
We walk with caution,
So we could get to the next step;
Still, we're falling.
And wake up in the morning,
Ask God what happened
During your sleeping break!
The criminals commit crimes everywhere,
Because they're careless!
Prisons are like shelters,
They don't care about it anymore!
Polices become soldiers,
Kill every day, everywhere
Just to protect themselves!
Who's going to protect us now?
In this situation, we need the help of God,
The one and only spirit
Who gave his Son's life for our Sins.
Earth is our planet,
And this is where we belong!
Now where else do you want us to go?
That is really scary.

Listen to my vwa!

I don't deal with brothers who don't like bon bagay!
Seating here, acting like ou pa konn mizè lakay!
Mwen se yon Ayisyen who don't like to get high...
While my Country Ayiti ap pase tray.

Mwen tankou yon zwazo who left home
To come to U.S k'ap spit me tankou lagoum.
Now, m'ap chache yon fucking broom
So, I could sweep off tout vye bagay nan lakou'm

N'ap rele aba Ministha!
You even forget se noumenm ki Mennen yo la.
I know you would say sa pa gade'w sa...
but this is all Haitians problem, even nou nan
diaspora.

Haiti was a beautiful peyi,
Avèk yon bann nèg smart, in poverty.
No food, vant yo ap ratresi
Like they're on diet po yo vin skinny!

My Country's been sold for diaman ak lò
By the government we trusted like Kapwa lanmò.
O Bondye, can you open another door?
So we could make Ayiti bèl like it was before.

We're the premye nwa's being free
Ki kounya in the top of misery!
Don't blame Americans, blame me!
Because mwen pa konn vale Ayiti!

60

If only you knew!

While you're asleep;
Do you know who protects you?
While you're at work;
Do you know who guides you?
While you're breathing;
I wonder if you think
About the others you made mad,
Confused, lost, cried, stress!
You can have three bad days,
Just thanks God you still alive.

Think for a moment,
Before you make your stupid move
Because everything has an end!
Life is more precious,
And it's very short.
You always think that you'll have
Time tomorrow,
Next time, or one day!

My heart is crying to tell you
If you only knew,
You might not return home.
You would definitively repent today!